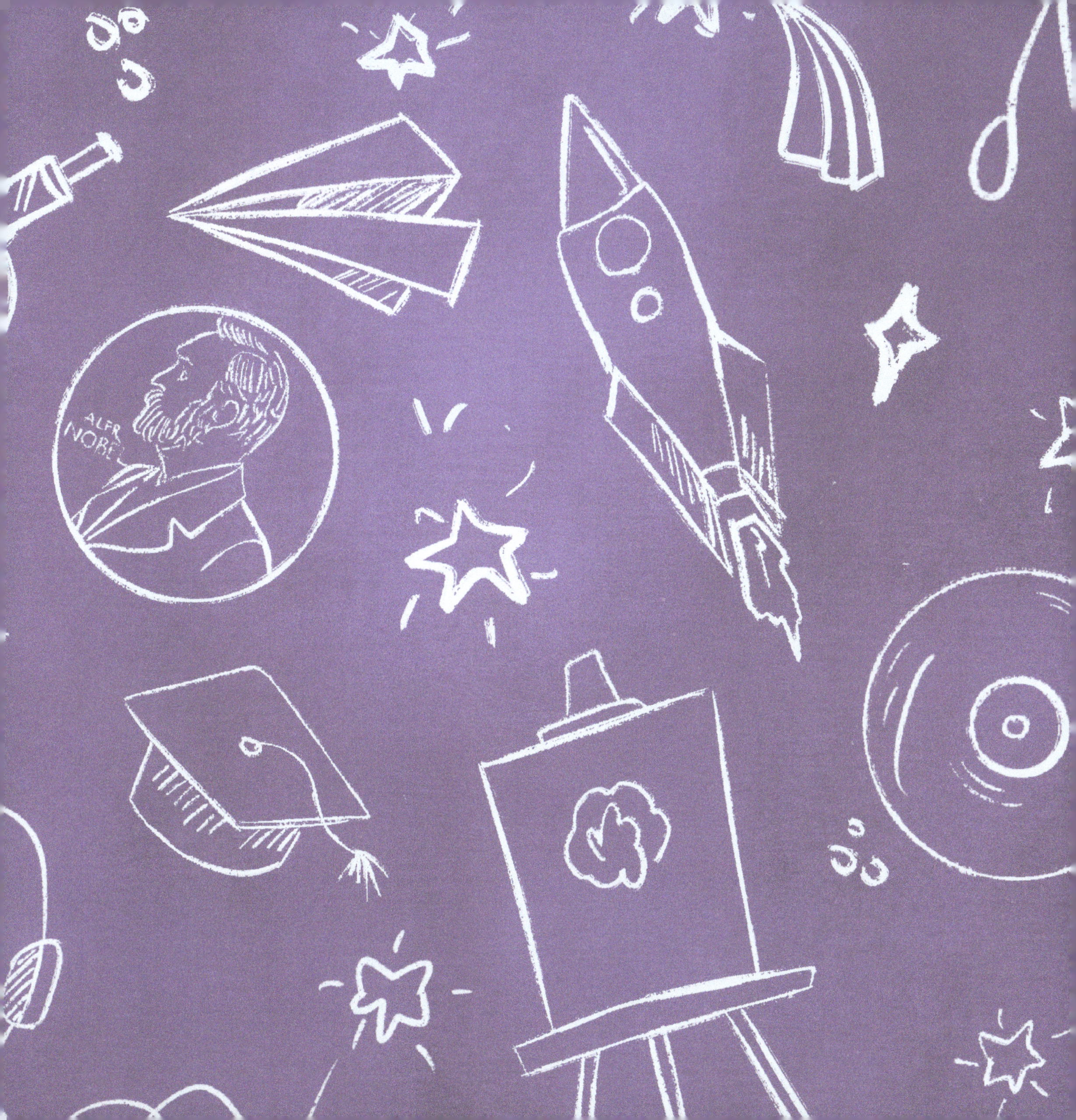
ALFR
NOBEL

Walt Disney

By Mary Nhin

Illustrated By
Yuliia Zolotova

Hi, I'm Walt Disney.

I loved to draw when I was a boy. In my free time, I copied cartoons from the newspapers.

I joined the school newspaper as our very own cartoonist. This is when my passion developed because I had a lot of fun doing it.

I developed my talent by taking night and weekend classes in art while I was in high school.

After finishing school, I became an artist's apprentice. Here, I drew cartoons for commercials, and eventually learned to work as an animator.

But opportunities for me were limited. This was shortly after World War I, when America was in the midst of the Great Depression. Many companies struggled financially, and I lost my job when my employer went out of business.

I was a talented cartoonist, but I had failed multiple times to set up my own cartoon companies after I lost my job.

All our dreams can come true,
if we have the courage to
pursue them.

HOLLYWOOD

Eventually I moved to Hollywood, deciding to have one more go at working for myself by setting up my own company. I founded the Walt Disney Company.

All the adversity I've had in my life, all my troubles and obstacles, have strengthened me. You may not realize it when it happens, but a kick in the teeth may be the best thing in the world for you.

Our very first animation starred Mickey Mouse, and it was one of the first cartoons to have sound.

Encouraged by the eventual success of our first animation, I was determined to produce a full color feature-length film.

It was a very large and expensive undertaking, and many in the industry were sure that we would fail. Nevertheless, we worked hard.

When our film launched, it was a huge success. The film was called *Snow White and the Seven Dwarves*, and it is still popular even today.

I became one of the biggest names in animation in the world and produced many more successful films. Nearly 100 years later, the Disney company is one of the largest entertainment companies in the world.

Whatever you do, do it well. Do it so well that when people see you do it, they will want to come back and see you do it again and they will want to bring others and show them how well you do what you do.

Timeline

1932 – Walt wins an Academy Award for Best
            Short Subject (Cartoon)

1960 – Walt is given two stars on the
            Hollywood Walk of Fame

1964 – Walt receives the Presidential
            Medal of Freedom

1968 – Walt is posthumously awarded the
            Congressional Gold Medal

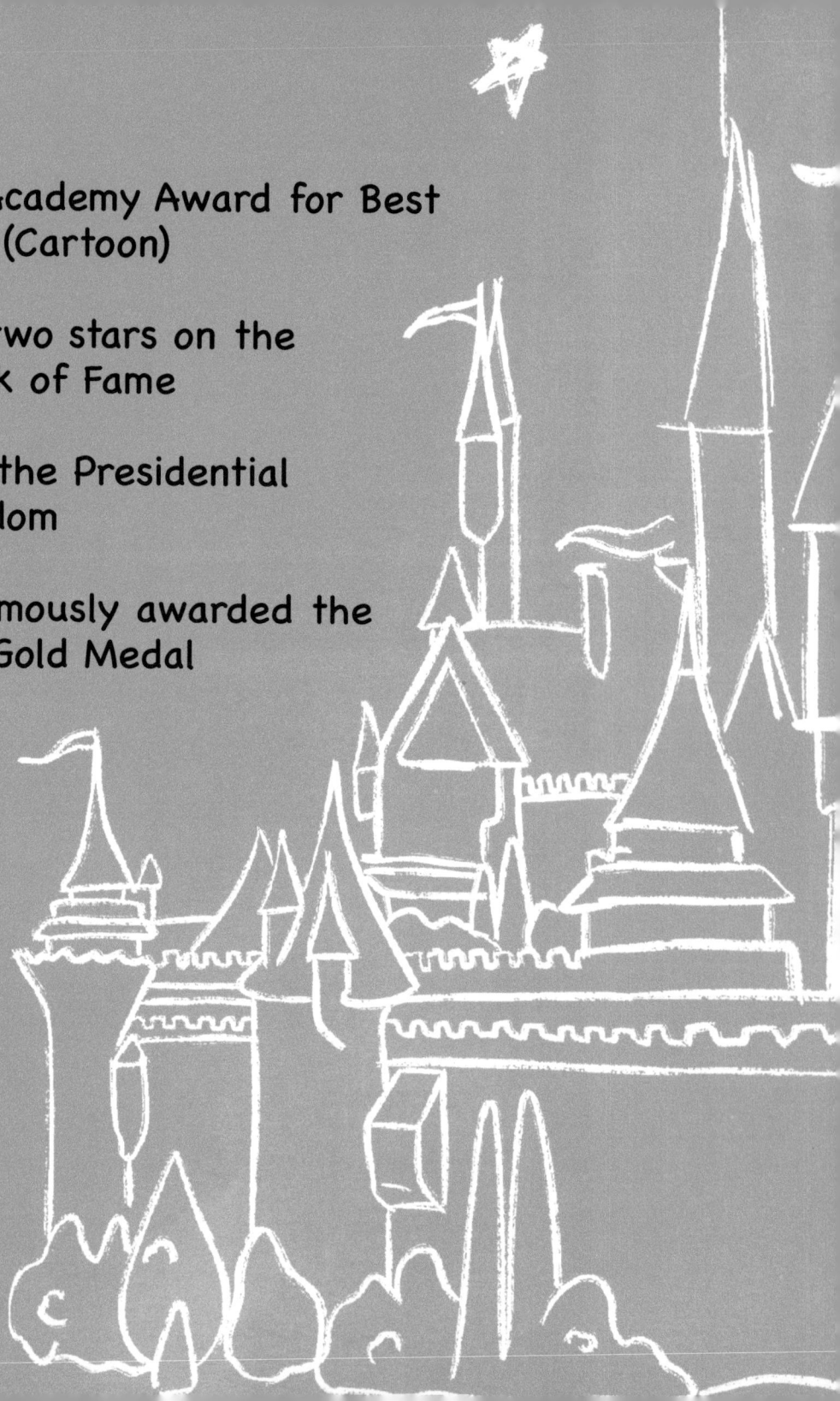

minimovers.tv

@marynhin   @GrowGrit
#minimoversandshakers

Mary Nhin   Ninja Life Hacks

Ninja Life Hacks

@marynhin

ALFR
NOBEL